SPOTLIGHT ON A FAIR AND EQUAL SOCIETY

RESPECTING OUR DIFFERENCES

RACHAEL MORLOCK

PowerKiDS press

Published in 2023 by The Rosen Publishing Group, Inc.
2544 Clinton Street, Buffalo, NY 14224

Copyright © 2023 by The Rosen Publishing Group, Inc.

All rights reserved. No part of this book may be reproduced in any form without permission in writing from the publisher, except by a reviewer.

First Edition

Editor: Greg Roza
Book Design: Michael Flynn

Photo Credits: Cover Viktorcvetkovic/iStock; (series background) tavizta/Shutterstock.com; p. 5 SAHACHATZ/Shutterstock.com; p. 6 p. 15 Rawpixel.com/Shutterstock.com/Shutterstock.com; p. 7 Monkey Business Images/Shutterstock.com; p. 9 Malivan_Iuliia/Shutterstock.com; p. 10 Torgado/Shutterstock.com; pp. 11, 18 Prostock-studio/Shutterstock.com; p. 13 Kathy Hutchins/Shutterstock.com; p. 14 Gonzalo Bell/Shutterstock.com; p. 15 Rawpixel.com/Shutterstock.com; p. 17 Ground Picture/Shutterstock.com; p. 19 vitstudio/Shutterstock.com; p. 21 Ryan Rahman/Shutterstock.com; p. 22 tomertu/Shutterstock.com; p. 23 MikeSaran/Shutterstock.com; p. 25 Drazen Zigic/Shutterstock.com; p. 26 Robert Kneschke/Shutterstock.com;
p. 27 AP Photo/JP; p. 29 Anastasia Mazeina/Shutterstock.com.

Library of Congress Cataloging-in-Publication Data

Names: Morlock, Rachael, author.
Title: Respecting our differences / Rachael Morlock.
Description: Buffalo, NY : PowerKids Press, [2023] | Series: Spotlight on a
   fair and equal society | Includes index.
Identifiers: LCCN 2022028231 (print) | LCCN 2022028232 (ebook) | ISBN
   9781538388280 (library binding) | ISBN 9781538388259 (paperback) | ISBN
   9781538388297 (ebook)
Subjects: LCSH: Social integration--Juvenile literature. |
   Equality--Juvenile literature.
Classification: LCC HM683 .M67 2023 (print) | LCC HM683 (ebook) | DDC
   302--dc23/eng/20220921
LC record available at https://lccn.loc.gov/2022028231
LC ebook record available at https://lccn.loc.gov/2022028232

Manufactured in the United States of America

Some of the images in this book illustrate individuals who are models. The depictions do not imply actual situations or events.

CPSIA Compliance Information: Batch #CWPK23. For further information contact Rosen Publishing at 1-800-237-9932.

CONTENTS

RESPECT 4
STARTING WITH IDENTITIES 6
DIVERSE COMMUNITIES 8
THAT'S NOT FAIR! 10
CHECK YOUR BIAS 12
ADVANTAGES AND DISADVANTAGES 14
FEELING DIFFERENT 16
RESPECTING RACIAL AND ETHNIC IDENTITY . . . 18
CELEBRATING CULTURE 20
RELIGIOUS BELIEFS 22
DIFFERENCES IN THE NEWS 24
PEOPLE WITH DISABILITIES 26
SHOWING RESPECT FOR FAMILY DIFFERENCES . . 28
HEALTHY COMMUNITIES 30
GLOSSARY 31
INDEX 32
PRIMARY SOURCES 32

CHAPTER ONE

RESPECT

Think about what respect means to you. How does a respectful person think and act? Respect is accepting someone as they are. To respect someone means choosing to act in a way that shows you listen to them. That choice comes from values and beliefs. You can respect people and things. You can respect a coach or a new neighbor. You can respect a public park, which means you treat it in the right way. Respect means that you recognize and value the rights, needs, or worth of each person, place, or thing.

Most often, showing respect gets respect from others. Students at one school made buttons with the simple words: "I choose respect." That means students who wore the buttons made a decision to be respectful in their words and actions. They decided to be self-aware and mindful of this choice. Respecting differences is a choice we all can make.

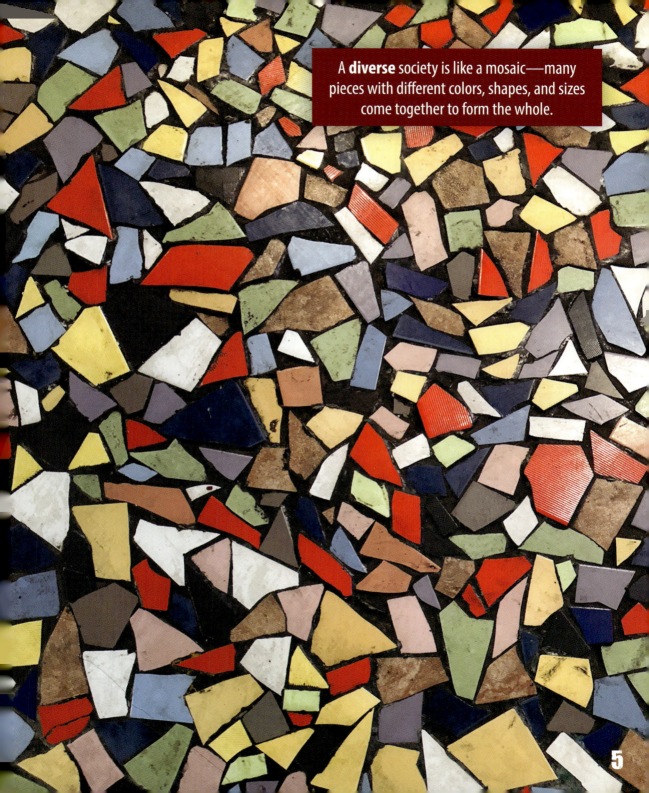

A **diverse** society is like a mosaic—many pieces with different colors, shapes, and sizes come together to form the whole.

CHAPTER TWO
STARTING WITH IDENTITIES

No two people are the same. We all have different beliefs, talents, cultures, values, life experiences, and features. These parts of who we are come together to form our identity.

Millions of **immigrants**—each with their own identity and way of life—have traveled to the United States in search of freedom.

Many different identities form a community, just as many different pieces come together to form a mosaic.

Some parts of identity have to do with personality. Your thoughts and feelings, the things you like and don't like, your strengths and weaknesses, your behavior, and what's important to you make up your personality. Parts of your personality may change over time.

You also have a social identity. This is the way you fit into the world. You're born with some parts of your social identity, and they may stay the same throughout your life. People around you have many different social identities that may include their race, ethnicity, culture, language, religion, **gender**, sexuality, body size, age, and abilities.

CHAPTER THREE

DIVERSE COMMUNITIES

We share our lives with other people in communities. Your class at school, sports team, neighborhood, or town are examples of communities. Communities can be places, or they can be groups of people with the same interests. The United States is a big nation made up of people with different identities living in many different kinds of communities.

Diverse communities have people with many social identities. Because of their separate backgrounds, they look, act, and think in ways that are different from each other. These differences make communities stronger.

We need differences in order to be creative and healthy. Where would new ideas come from if everyone thought in the same way? Differences can also be exciting! When you're part of a diverse community, you learn to see the world from new **perspectives** with respectful eyes.

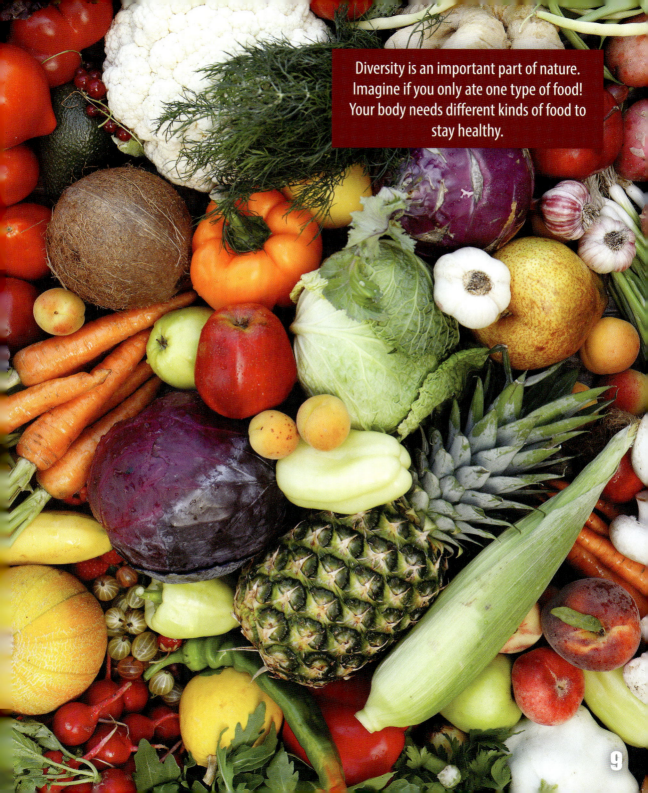

Diversity is an important part of nature. Imagine if you only ate one type of food! Your body needs different kinds of food to stay healthy.

CHAPTER FOUR
THAT'S NOT FAIR!

Some people feel nervous when they see people who look or act differently from them. When people think that their own identity is best, they can react to differences with **negative** thoughts and emotions. The truth is, no social identity is better than any other.

Muslim students are bullied twice as much as other students. Bullying is not fair. It makes people feel like who they are is strange or wrong.

Believing that your identity is best or right can lead you to treat other people unfairly. This kind of unfair treatment is called discrimination. Bullying based on someone's identity is one kind of discrimination.

Discrimination is also bigger than what happens between people. It means that members of some groups don't have the same opportunities as other people. This makes it difficult for them to go to school, visit a doctor, find a place to live, get a job, or elect lawmakers who consider their needs when creating new laws.

CHAPTER FIVE
CHECK YOUR BIAS

A stereotype is an idea about a group of people. Many people think this idea is true—but it isn't. People may believe a sterotype about a specific group and reject the fact that it is not true or only partly true.

It's easy to start believing stereotypes without even realizing it. They come in messages from family members, teachers, television, movies, books, leaders, and society in general. If stereotypes cause you to think positively or negatively about a social group, that's called bias.

Stereotypes are harmful because they make all members of a group seem the same. That doesn't leave room for people to be themselves. Negative bias can keep people from getting what they need or achieving their goals. Your biases can hurt you, too, by limiting how you see others. Speak up respectfully when you see bias in action, and treat all people as individuals.

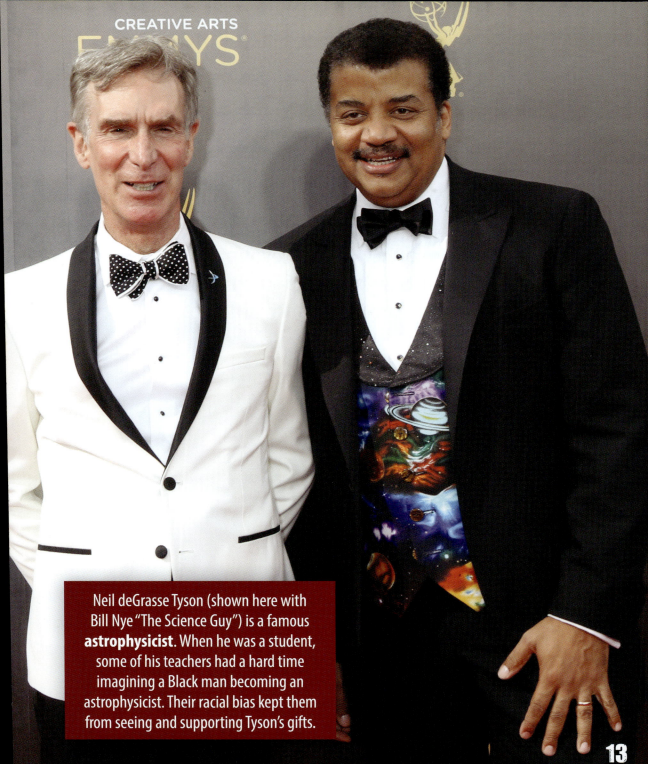

Neil deGrasse Tyson (shown here with Bill Nye "The Science Guy") is a famous **astrophysicist**. When he was a student, some of his teachers had a hard time imagining a Black man becoming an astrophysicist. Their racial bias kept them from seeing and supporting Tyson's gifts.

CHAPTER SIX

ADVANTAGES AND DISADVANTAGES

Some people have unfair advantages. Some have unfair disadvantages. Often these are based on who they are and where they were born. Advantages help you to succeed and meet your needs; they work for you. Disadvantages are often barriers to success.

A path to success in life can start with a community that meets the needs of its children.

    Families with advantages might live in communities with good schools. Quality schools lead to opportunities for success in college or other training, and that can lead to good jobs. Good jobs create more advantages in life.
    Raising a family in a community with schools that fail to support students can be a serious disadvantage. Schools may not meet learners' needs for many reasons, but poverty plays a big part. Learners who can't succeed in school have disadvantages in getting good jobs or reaching higher education. It is much harder to reach your goals no matter how hard you work.

CHAPTER SEVEN

FEELING DIFFERENT

How does it feel to be different? Since our identities are made up of many parts, everyone feels different sometimes. Your differences can make you feel proud or excited. Other times, feeling different can be lonely or challenging.

Feeling **empathy** for people who are left out, mistreated, or ashamed because of their identity is an opportunity to support them. You may experience hurtful actions or words because of an aspect of your identity. Talking with someone you trust can help you understand where the feeling comes from and how to deal with it. Naming your emotions is a good start.

Diversity is a part of human life. Talking about it helps us appreciate our differences and build strong connections with each other.

One way to show respect is to listen carefully when others talk about their identity and life experiences.

CHAPTER EIGHT

RESPECTING RACIAL AND ETHNIC IDENTITY

A look at kids in U.S. schools in fall 2019 shows an interesting trend. That fall, kids from racial and ethnic minority groups were more than half the population in public schools. Hispanic, Black, and Asian American students, for the first time, made up the majority population in schools. In 1995, kids from these groups made up about a third of school populations.

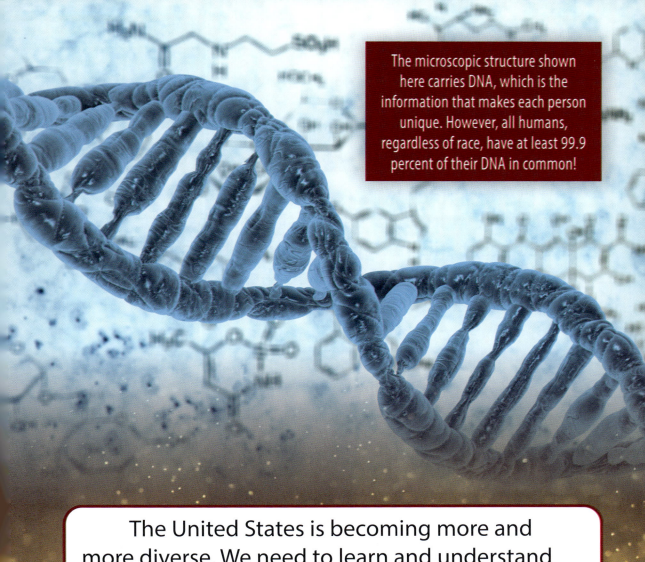

The microscopic structure shown here carries DNA, which is the information that makes each person unique. However, all humans, regardless of race, have at least 99.9 percent of their DNA in common!

    The United States is becoming more and more diverse. We need to learn and understand more about racial and ethnic identities.

    With goals of respect and fairness, we can work past issues in which some people believe one racial identity is better than others. White people, once the majority, still have many advantages that are unfair.

CHAPTER NINE
CELEBRATING CULTURE

Some differences in identity are based on culture. Culture is the set of **customs**, arts, languages, beliefs, foods, and practices shared by a group of people. Many people are proud of their unique cultures.

Ethnic groups may share the same language, history, and origins. For example, those of Hispanic ethnicity are people whose families come from Spanish-speaking countries. Ethnicity ties similar people together with a shared culture that can be celebrated.

Celebrating different cultures can start with learning more about the cultures of your family. Next, try finding out more about the cultures of your friends and classmates. Some fun ways of exploring many cultures include going to festivals, trying ethnic foods, reading world folk tales, and learning a new language.

In the United States, many different ethnic and cultural groups are described with a compound name to show the way their cultural heritage is blended with an American identity, as in "Mexican American."

CHAPTER TEN
RELIGIOUS BELIEFS

Another part of identity is religion. Religion is a system of beliefs, behaviors, and moral values. Religious and nonreligious beliefs may help people decide what matters in life and how to act. Many of the world's religions share a belief that we should be kind and fair to others, take care of those in need, be honest, and do the right thing. Even if you don't agree with certain beliefs, you can show respect for the people who hold them.

During Hanukkah, Jewish people light candles in a candle holder called a menorah, shown here. As of 2020, there are more than 7 million Jewish people in the United States.

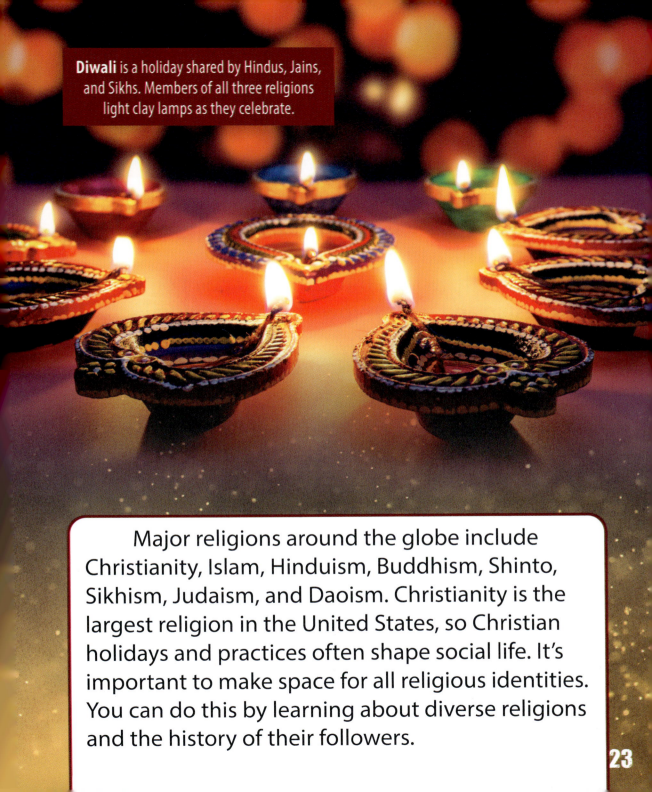

Diwali is a holiday shared by Hindus, Jains, and Sikhs. Members of all three religions light clay lamps as they celebrate.

Major religions around the globe include Christianity, Islam, Hinduism, Buddhism, Shinto, Sikhism, Judaism, and Daoism. Christianity is the largest religion in the United States, so Christian holidays and practices often shape social life. It's important to make space for all religious identities. You can do this by learning about diverse religions and the history of their followers.

CHAPTER ELEVEN

DIFFERENCES IN THE NEWS

You can often see people's problems with differences reflected in news reports. Religious differences may trigger anger and conflict. People may express this hate through spray paint on places of worship and rocks thrown through windows. People in some neighborhoods may not welcome those from different ethnic groups. Hurtful speech on social media can cause fighting in schools. During the COVID-19 **pandemic**, differences over mask rules resulted in anger and harmful actions.

Some news stories about differences are positive. People of one religion may help refugees of another religion. Some stories may show people defeating stereotypes, such as a woman coaching for a Major League Baseball team. A neighborhood's people may come together to celebrate diverse winter holidays, sharing food, customs, and new experiences. School communities may help students through volunteer mentoring and supplying computers.

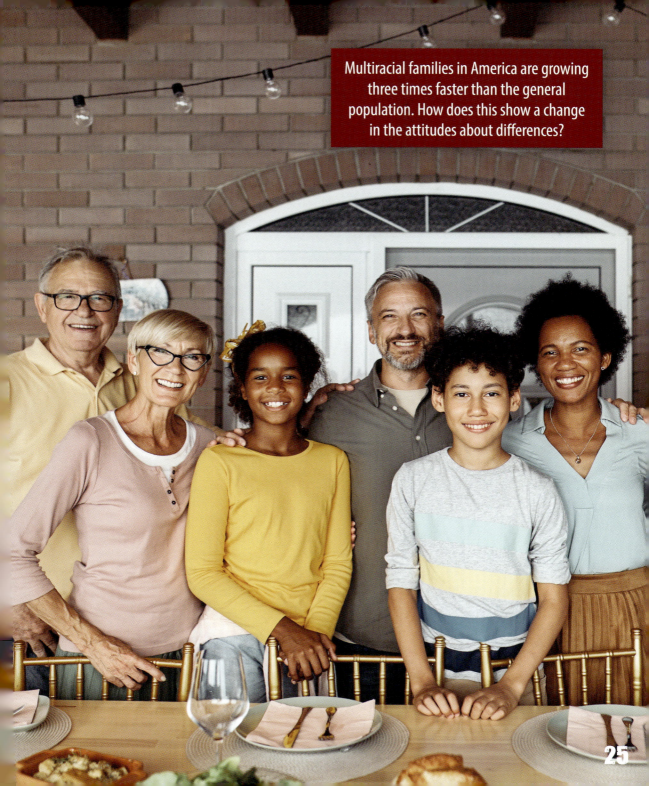

Multiracial families in America are growing three times faster than the general population. How does this show a change in the attitudes about differences?

CHAPTER TWELVE
PEOPLE WITH DISABILITIES

Another way that humans differ from each other is in their abilities. A disability is a condition that affects the way someone moves, communicates, thinks, learns, or feels in their daily life. Some people are born with a disability and others may become disabled later. In the United States, more than 61 million adults and 7 million students have a disability.

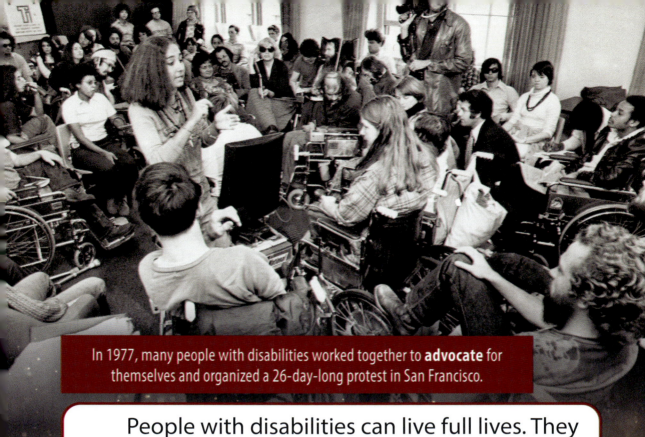

In 1977, many people with disabilities worked together to **advocate** for themselves and organized a 26-day-long protest in San Francisco.

People with disabilities can live full lives. They have many gifts and skills to share. However, many barriers, including a lack of understanding, still stand in people's way. Solutions to these problems include more support for those with disabilities and more training to help others understand. Disability **activists** work to make society more **accessible**. The Americans with Disabilities Act and other laws supporting educational opportunities help protect the rights of people with disabilities and make **inclusion** more common.

CHAPTER THIRTEEN
SHOWING RESPECT FOR FAMILY DIFFERENCES

No matter who you are, you can celebrate diversity by showing respect for others. We are all different, but we all have similarities that draw us together too. Families can differ from one another in many ways, but they're often still the heart of our identity. Some families have a mom, dad, and kids. Many families are thriving with a single parent or a grandparent. Some families have two moms or two dads. Kids can be born into families or adopted and thrive in a loving home. Sometimes new families grow because marriages connect two people who are already parents.

You can build the words and knowledge you need to welcome everyone's family. You can learn and listen to the ways people talk about themselves, their families, and their community.

Families are diverse and come in all shapes and sizes.

CHAPTER FOURTEEN
HEALTHY COMMUNITIES

You can celebrate diversity in your community and in the larger world. Look for stories from people with different identities from your own. When you imagine life from another person's perspective, you practice empathy and move toward **compassion** and action. Empathy is feeling the emotions, thoughts, and experiences of others. It can help you build true friendships and see everyone as part of one large community.

Celebrating differences means understanding the colorful mosaic of identities that make up your community. Similarities and differences are everywhere. Each person has their own identity, but they are also part of the human family. The strongest communities are built by people who feel united by what they have in common, comfortable sharing their differences, and willing to work for everyone's rights.

GLOSSARY

accessible (ik-SEH-suh-buhl) Easy to obtain, use, or understand.

activist (AK-tih-vist) Someone who acts strongly in support of or against an issue.

advocate (AD-vuh-kayt) To support or argue for a cause or policy.

astrophysicist (as-troh-FIH-suh-zihst) A scientist who specializes in studying space, stars, planets, and the universe.

compassion (kuhm-PAA-shun) A feeling of sympathy and a desire to help.

custom (KUH-stuhm) An action or way of behaving that's traditional among the people in a certain group or place.

diverse (diy-VUHRS) Having many different types, forms, or ideas.

Diwali (duh-WAH-lee) A Hindu festival of lights held late in October.

empathy (EHM-puh-thee) The understanding and sharing of the emotions and experiences of another person.

gender (JEN-duhr) The set of social expectations or traits men or women are expected to meet or have.

immigrant (IH-muh-grunt) A person who comes to a country to live there.

inclusion (in-KLOO-zhuhn) The act of including and integrating all people and groups.

negative (NEH-guh-tiv) Harmful, bad, or unwanted.

pandemic (pan-DEH-mihk) An outbreak of a disease that occurs over a wide geographic area and typically affects a significant proportion of the population.

perspective (puhr-SPEK-tiv) Point of view.

INDEX

B
bias, 12, 13

C
communities, 7, 8, 15, 30
COVID-19 pandemic, 24
cultures, 6, 7, 20, 21

D
disabilities, 24, 25
discrimination, 11
Diwali, 23

H
Hanukkah, 22

I
identity, 6, 7, 8, 10, 11, 16, 17, 19, 20, 21, 22, 23, 28

R
religion, 22, 23, 24

S
social identity, 7, 8, 10
stereotype, 12, 24

T
Tyson, Neil Degrasse, 13

U
United States, 8, 18, 19, 21, 23, 26

PRIMARY SOURCES

Page 6
Statue of Liberty. Welcome to the land of freedom - An ocean steamer passing the Statue of Liberty: Scene on the steerage deck. Engraving. Ca. 1887. Part of the Everett Collection.

Page 13
Neil deGrasse Tyson (right) is shown with Bill Nye at the 2016 Primetime Creative Emmy Awards. Photograph. September 11, 2016. Los Angeles, CA. Held by Shutterstock.

Page 27
Protest by disability activists. Photograph. April 9, 1977. San Francisco, CA. Held by Shutterstock.